TICKET TO THE
BOSTON MARATHON

MARTIN GITLIN

45TH PARALLEL PRESS

Published in the United States of America by Cherry Lake Publishing Group
Ann Arbor, Michigan
www.cherrylakepublishing.com

Reading Adviser: Reading Advisor: Beth Walker Gambro, MS Ed., Reading Consultant, Yorkville, IL.

Photo Credits: © AP Photo/Winslow Townson, cover; © Mr. Beekeeper/Shutterstock, cover page; © Nosyrevy/Shutterstock, 2, 3, 6, 10, 16, 23, 32; © AndrewNoiles/Shutterstock, 5; © Marcio Jose Bastos Silva/Shutterstock, 7; Anonymous unknown author, Public domain, via Wikimedia Commons, 9; © Marcos Souza/Dreamstime.com, 11; © Michalk/Shutterstock, 12; © Art Merch X/Shuttterstock, 13, 19, 25, 28; Agence Rol, Public domain, via Wikimedia Commons, 15; Bibliothèque nationale de France, Public Domain, via Wikimedia Commons, 17; © Marcio Jose Bastos Silva/Shutterstock, 18; © Icon Sportswire via AP Images/ASSOCIATED PRESS, 21; © James Kirkikis/Shutterstock, 22; Governor's Press Office, Massachusetts, Public Domain via Wikimedia Commons, 24, 27; Gianina Lindsey, CC BY 2.0 via Wikimedia Commons, 28

Copyright © 2026 by Cherry Lake Publishing Group

All rights reserved. No part of this book may be reproduced or utilized in any
form or by any means without written permission from the publisher.

45th Parallel Press is an imprint of Cherry Lake Publishing Group.

Library of Congress Cataloging-in-Publication Data

Names: Gitlin, Marty author
Title: Ticket to the Boston Marathon / by Martin Gitlin.
Description: Ann Arbor, Michigan : 45th Parallel Press, 2025. | Series: The
  big game | Audience: Grades 7-9 | Summary: "Who has won the Boston
  Marathon? How did they make it happen? Filled with high-interest text
  written with struggling readers in mind, this series includes fun facts,
  intriguing stories, and captivating play-by-plays from one of the most
  famous marathons in the world"-- Provided by publisher.
Identifiers: LCCN 2025009134 | ISBN 9781668963852 hardcover | ISBN
  9781668965177 paperback | ISBN 9781668966785 ebook | ISBN 9781668968390
  pdf
Subjects: LCSH: Boston Marathon--History--Juvenile literature |
  Long-distance runners--Biography--Juvenile literature
Classification: LCC GV1065.22.B67 G57 2025 | DDC
  796.42/520974461--dc23/eng/20250417
LC record available at https://lccn.loc.gov/2025009134

Cherry Lake Publishing Group would like to acknowledge the work of the Partnership for 21st Century Learning,
a Network of Battelle for Kids. Please visit Battelle for Kids online for more information.

Printed in the United States of America

Note from publisher: Websites change regularly, and their future contents are outside of our control.
Supervise children when conducting any recommended online searches for extended learning opportunities.

Table of Contents

Introduction 4

History of the Game 8

Early Days, Big Moments 14

Modern Moments 20

Rising Stars 26

ACTIVITY 30

LEARN MORE 30

GLOSSARY 31

INDEX 32

ABOUT THE AUTHOR 32

Introduction

It is the third Monday in April. Runners line up in Boston, Massachusetts. They have come from around the world.

More than 30,000 racers are ready. They are about to run the most famous **marathon** in the world. That is a 26.2-mile (42.2 kilometer) race. It is the Boston Marathon.

A marathon is a test of **endurance**. Endurance is the ability to keep going. Being able to finish is a big achievement. People train for months. They train for years.

The waiting is over and the big race is about to begin. Get ready, running fans!

Most do it for fun. They just want to finish. Many try hard to win. Those are the best runners. They often run many marathons every year. Some race all over the world. There are even wheelchair racers. About 50 complete the course in wheelchairs.

The race is held in any weather. There has been snow. There has been driving rain. There has been severe heat. All of these things can make the race harder. But runners run no matter what. They test themselves. They prove themselves. They go the distance.

Let the big race begin!

Marathon runners are grateful for support from the sidelines.

History of the Game

John Graham attended the first modern Olympics. He was the U.S. Olympic team manager. That was in 1896. Those Olympics were held in Athens, Greece. Among its events was a marathon. And Graham was inspired.

Graham loved the marathon. He was from Boston. He wanted to start a marathon there. So he went to work. Graham looked for a good **route**. That is a race path for runners. He found one. The first Boston Marathon was set. It would take place on April 19, 1897.

Only 18 runners entered. John McDermott won. He was from New York. The race was just 24.8 miles (39.9 km). It was not expanded to 26.2 miles (42.2 km) until 1924.

Coverage of the first-ever Boston Marathon in *The Boston Globe*, April 20, 1897

April 19 is a holiday in Massachusetts. It is Patriots' Day. It marks the start of the Revolutionary War. And it was the **annual** date of the Boston Marathon, unless it fell on a Sunday. Annual means something happens every year.

That continued through 1968. The date changed in 1969. It is now held every third Monday in April.

The Marathon has evolved. No woman raced until Roberta Gibb in 1966. But she ran it secretly. Gibb hid in the bushes. Then she joined the race.

Katherine Switzer ran in 1967. She signed up using her initials. An official ran after her. He tried to take her bib. Male runners stopped him. They stood up for their fellow runner. Women were not officially allowed to run until 1972. Eight women ran that year. All of them finished.

The Wheelchair Division began in 1975. The first man to complete the Boston Marathon in a wheelchair was Bob Hall. He finished the race in 2 hours, 58 minutes.

For more than 50 years now, women have run the Boston Marathon with pride.

The Boston Marathon slowly grew. Runners from around the world joined.

Runners have gotten much faster. When John McDermott won in 1897, his time was nearly 3 hours. The fastest Open Division time was recorded in 2011. That was run by Geoffrey Mutai. He is from the country of Kenya. That is in Africa. He finished the race in 2 hours, 3 minutes, and 2 seconds.

Geoffrey Mutai on his way to set a world record time for the Boston Marathon in 2011

Who is going to win the Boston Marathon? Usually nobody knows. But not when Bill Rodgers was running. It was assumed he would win.

Rodgers was among the best marathon racers ever. It began in 1975. That was his first Boston victory. Rodgers finished in 2 hours, 10 minutes.

He was just warming up. Rodgers won 3 Boston Marathons straight, starting in 1978. He even broke his own record in 1979. That is when he ran it in 2 hours, 9 minutes, and 27 seconds.

Rodgers peaked in 1978. He won 27 of 30 races he entered. Rodgers won the New York Marathon. He took the Fukuoka Marathon. That is in Japan. He was simply the best in the world.

Early Days, Big Moments

The most amazing Marathon runner ever? It might have been Clarence DeMar. He was born in Ohio in 1888. DeMar ran his first Boston Marathon in 1910. He finished second.

That is where the story begins. DeMar got bad news in 1911. He was told he had a heart problem. Doctors told him not to race anymore. But he did anyway. And he won the Marathon that year.

DeMar then stopped racing. It seemed he was done as a runner. But he ran the Marathon in 1917. Then he started up again in 1922. He was 33 years old. Nobody expected much.

Even heart problems could not stop Clarence DeMar from running—and winning!

DeMar was about to shock the world. He won the Marathon in 1922. Then he became a legend. He finished first again in 1923. DeMar was the first 3-time winner. And he was just getting started.

In 1924 he hurt himself in the race. DeMar jumped over a snowdrift. The result was hip and back pain. But he pushed through. DeMar won that Marathon, too. He had won 3 in a row. He ran it in 1924 in 2 hours, 29 minutes. It was the fastest time yet. One reporter called him "a Superman."

DeMar won it again in 1927. And 1928. And 1930. His last win was at age 41. He remains the only 7-time winner of the Open Division.

Jean Driscoll was another Boston Marathon star. She raced 60 years after DeMar. But she didn't run. She wheeled! Driscoll first won the Wheelchair Division in 1990. And she kept winning. She finished first 7 straight years! Her last victory was in 2000. That was her 8th win.

DeMar kept winning the Boston Marathon despite pain.

Driscoll was born with spina bifida. This condition is when the spine never fully develops. Driscoll struggled with walking. She had to use a wheelchair.

She stayed active. She played wheelchair basketball. And she raced. Driscoll was in 3 **Paralympics**. That is a sporting event for people with disabilities. Driscoll even won 5 gold medals. She won the last one in 2000.

The women's wheelchair division has been part of the Marathon since 1977.

The United States and Canada once **dominated** the men's Marathon. That means their runners won it every year. No runner from another country won from 1897 to 1919.

Then along came Peter Trivoulidis. He was from Greece. Trivoulidis won the 1920 event. He actually lived in New York City. He moved from Greece in 1914. But he still represented his native country.

It was not a trend. Runners from the United States and Canada kept winning. International runners broke through around 1946. And they have recently dominated.

WAY BACK WHEN

Modern Moments

Peres Jepchirchir had a tough life. She was born in Kenya. That is a country in Africa. She was raised on a tiny farm. Her family was poor. They could not afford to send her to school. She had to drop out.

So she ran. She ran to forget her struggles. Jepchirchir ran long distances. And she got fast. Jepchirchir helped Kenya win 2 gold medals at the World Half Marathon Championships.

She peaked in 2022. Jepchirchir had already won Olympic gold. Then she won the New York Marathon. Jepchirchir was ready for Boston. She did not just win that. She ran it in 2 hours, 21 minutes. That was the fastest time in 8 years.

Peres Jepchirchir ran her way to Boston Marathon greatness.

Japanese runner Kawauchi broke a streak of African dominance at the 2018 Marathon.

Four years earlier, something else great happened. It was 2018. The weather in Boston was awful. It was rainy. It was windy. It was cold. Nobody could run as fast as usual. Marathon times were slow. But Yuki Kawauchi did something amazing.

African runners had been dominating. They had won all but 2 events since 1991. Kawauchi was from Japan. He was not expected to win. But he did.

Kawauchi was used to racing in bad weather. He had already won one race in freezing weather. So he was ready for Boston. His winning time was the slowest since 1976. But that did not matter. He was still the champion.

Champions can come from all over the world. Take Marcel Hug for example. He is from Switzerland. He is fast. He is the greatest wheelchair racer around.

Hug showed how fast he could be in the Boston Marathon Wheelchair Division. He won his first Boston Marathon in 2015. His time was 1 hour, 29 minutes. Then he kept winning. He won it 8 times in 10 years.

Swiss wheelchair racer Marcel Hug got faster and faster to win 7 races.

But Hug got even faster. He finished in 2024 at 1 hour, 15 minutes, and 33 seconds. That was not only the winning time. It was the fastest ever in Boston.

Not even Hug could beat that score the next year. He finished at 1 hour, 21 minutes, and 34 seconds in 2025.

In 2013, the Boston Marathon Bombing happened. Two men planted bombs. They set them in the crowd. Three people died. Hundreds were hurt. The tragedy is remembered. The victims are honored.

The tragedy brought Boston together. Its mayor spoke about pride for his city. People in Boston embraced his words. They too loved their city. And they were proud of how it recovered.

Rising Stars

Keep an eye on these rising stars. They might soon become legends!

Eden Rainbow-Cooper

Boston Marathon winners are rarely young. That is true in all divisions. But Eden Rainbow-Cooper was different. She won the wheelchair race in 2024. She was only 23 years old.

Rainbow-Cooper is from England. She was born with sacral agenesis. It is a rare spine disease. It prevented Rainbow-Cooper from walking. But it did not stop her from racing. She began at age 12.

Victories soon followed. She won two 2022 wheelchair races in England. Then Rainbow-Cooper won the 2024 event in Boston. She finished in 1 hour, 35 minutes, and 11 seconds.

Eden Rainbow-Cooper's 2024 winning Boston Marathon time was 30 seconds ahead of her closest competitor's time.

One runner cheated to win the Boston Marathon. That was Rosie Ruiz in 1980.

The real winner was Jacqueline Gareau. She was from Canada. Gareau trained hard for the event. She was an unknown. Nobody believed she could win. But she passed the finish line first. At least that is what she thought.

Suddenly she saw a sad sight. Rosie Ruiz was being crowned with a laurel wreath. It is given to Marathon winners. What was going on? How could she have won without cheating?

She hadn't. Ruiz had slipped into the race near the end. Nobody even noticed. A week later, it was found she had cheated. And Gareau was handed the crown.

A BIT OF TRIVIA

Briar-Rose Honeywill-Sykes

Briar-Rose Honeywill-Sykes was lucky. She had a lucky birthday. She turned 18 on April 14, 2024. It qualified her for the 2024 women's Boston Marathon. The event was held the next day.

It's quite the comeback story. Honeywill-Sykes had COVID-19 in 2022. She could not work out. Injuries stopped her again in 2024. She was on crutches.

Honeywill-Sykes refused to give up. She was finally allowed to run in the Boston Marathon. She was the youngest woman ever to finish the race. It was a great day she would never forget.

Jacqueline Gareau was still running in 2013 at the Mount Washington Road Race.

Activity

Create your own Boston Marathon runner bio. Study the race's history. With an adult, go online. Look for past winners. Pick out your favorite. It could be a man or woman. Then find out more about that person.

Write down all the information you find. Find out where that winner was from. Learn about how that person trained for the event. Study what inspired the winner to be great. Talk to a grown up or teacher about writing a biography. Or research how to write one on your own.

Ask yourself why you chose that winner. Then start with writing 100 words about the person. Show what you write. Talk about it with friends and family. Add to your runner's biography over time. It might even spur an interest in running.

Learn More

BOOKS

Orr, Tamra B. *Boston: History, People, Landmarks: Fenway Park, Boston Common, Paul Revere.* Mount Joy, PA: Curious Fox Books, 2024.

Petersen, Justin. *Boston Marathon.* La Jolla, CA: Scobre Educational, 2015.

Williams, Heather. 2013 *Boston Marathon.* Ann Arbor, MI: Cherry Lake Publishing, 2019.

WEBSITES

Search these online sources with an adult.

ESPN | 26.2 facts about the Boston Marathon

Sports Illustrated for Kids | Boston Marathon: An Amazing 26.2 Miles

Marathon Kids: Kids Running

Glossary

annual (AN-yoo-wuhl) once every year

endurance (in-DUHR-uhns) the ability to keep going for a long time, especially when it is hard

dominated (DAH-muh-nay-tuhd) won easily or by a large margin

marathon (MAIR-uh-thahn) race of 26.2 miles (42.2 km)

Paralympics (per-uh-LIM-piks) sporting event for athletes with disabilities

route (ROOT) path a race is run from start to finish

spectators (SPEK-tay-tuhrz) people attending a sporting event in person

Index

A
activities, 30
ages, athletes, 14, 16, 26, 29

B
bombing (2013), 13
Bostonians, 10, 13
Boston Marathon
athletes, 4–12, 14–30
history, 8–12, 16, 19
route, 8

C
cheating, 28

D
DeMar, Clarence, 14–18
Driscoll, Jean, 18

G
Gareau, Jacqueline, 28–29
Gibb, Roberta, 10
Graham, John, 8

H
Hall. Bob, 10
Honeywill-Sykes, Briar-Rose, 29
Hug, Marcel, 24

I
international athletes, 12, 19–23, 26–28

J
Jepchirchir, Peres, 20–21

K
Kawauchi, Yuki, 22–23

M
MacDonald, Ronald, 12
marathons, 4–6, 8, 20, 25
McDermott, John, 8–9, 12
Mutai, Geoffrey, 12

O
Olympics and Paralympics, 8, 18, 20

R
Rainbow-Cooper, Eden, 26–27
Rodgers, Bill, 25
Ruiz, Rosie, 29

S
speeds, 12, 16, 20, 23–27

T
terrorist attacks, 13
Trivoulidis, Peter, 19

W
weather, 12, 22–23
wheelchair events, 6, 10, 18, 24, 26–27
winners, 8, 10, 12, 16–27, 28

About the Author

Martin Gitlin is an educational book author based in Connecticut. He won more than 45 awards as a newspaper sportswriter from 1991 to 2002. Included was a first-place award from the Associated Press for his coverage of the 1995 World Series. He has had more than 200 books published since 2006. Most of them were written for students.